PIRANHAS

Rachel Lynette

PowerKiDS
press

New York

Published in 2013 by The Rosen Publishing Group, Inc.
29 East 21st Street, New York, NY 10010

First Edition

Editor: Jennifer Way
Book Design: Greg Tucker

Photo Credits: Cover DEA/C. Bevilacqua/De Agostini Picture Library/Getty Images; p. 4 Maxim Tupikov/Shutterstock.com; p. 5 Bill Kennedy/Shutterstock.com; p. 6 Mark Smith/Photo Researchers/Getty Images; p. 7 Janne Hamalainen/Shutterstock.com; p. 8 Jupiterimages/Photos.com/Thinkstock; p. 9 Ed Reschke/Peter Arnold/Getty Images; p. 10 Altrendo Travel/Getty Images; p. 11 (left) © Flirt/Superstock; p. 11 (bottom) Zdorov Kirill Vladimirovich/Shutterstock.com; pp. 12–13 Lightpoet/Shutterstock.com; p. 14 Lehakok/Shutterstock.com; p. 15 Panache Productions/Oxford Scientific/Getty Images; p. 16 iStockphoto/Thinkstock; p. 17 Ishara S. Kodikara/AFP/Getty Images; p. 18–19 Prill Mediendesign und Fotografie/Shutterstock.com; p. 20 Fritz Poelking/age fotostock/Getty Images; p. 21 (top) © Nomad/Superstock; p. 21 (bottom) Berndt Fischer/Oxford Scientific/Getty Images; p. 22 Tepic/Shutterstock.com.

Library of Congress Cataloging-in-Publication Data

Lynette, Rachel.
  Piranhas / by Rachel Lynette. — 1st ed.
      p. cm. — (Monsters of the animal kingdom)
  Includes index.
  ISBN 978-1-4488-9634-9 (library binding) — ISBN 978-1-4488-9723-0 (pbk.) —
  ISBN 978-1-4488-9724-7 (6-pack)
  1. Piranhas—Juvenile literature. I. Title.
  QL638.C5L963 2013
  597'.48—dc23
                                    2012020041

Manufactured in the United States of America

CPSIA Compliance Information: Batch #W13PK5: For Further Information contact Rosen Publishing, New York, New York at 1-800-237-9932

CONTENTS

FEROCIOUS FISH

Imagine seeing a school of small fish attacking a cow that has been thrown into the water. The fish eat the cow until there is nothing left but bone just a few minutes later! That is what President Theodore Roosevelt saw in 1913. The fish he saw were piranhas, but what Roosevelt saw was a very

Most of the time, piranhas eat smaller fish. Some species even eat plants.

The red-bellied piranha, shown here, is named for the reddish color that adults have on their undersides.

rare event. The feeding frenzy he saw happens only when a group of starving piranhas is trapped together in a small space.

There are 33 **species** of piranhas. The red-bellied piranha is the best known. It is also one of the more common species.

RIVER FISH

Piranhas can be found in all of the major rivers in South America, including the Amazon. Since piranhas need to live in warm water, they do not live in cooler mountain rivers.

The black-spot piranha, shown here, lives in the Orinoco River in Venezuela.

In piranhas' South American habitat, there is a wet season and a dry season. During the wet season, rivers may overflow their banks, taking the piranhas with them. Some piranhas get trapped in small ponds formed by the flooding. During the dry season, these ponds shrink. Many piranhas die in these ponds before the wet season comes around again.

The Orinoco River flows through Venezuela and Colombia. It is one of South America's major river systems.

7

BUILT TO KILL

Piranhas are not large fish. Black piranhas are the biggest species, and they are only 2 feet (60 cm) long. Most piranhas are closer to 8 inches (20 cm) long.

Piranhas are built to attack **prey** by biting it. Their flat, plate-shaped bodies make it easy for them to dodge quickly when attacking and to avoid bumping into other

This is a piranha's eye. Scientists believe that piranhas can see nearby objects well, but that they have poor long-distance vision.

This piranha's flat body allows the fish to swim in a tight pack with fellow piranhas.

fish in the school. They have an excellent sense of smell. A piranha can smell a single drop of blood in more than 50 gallons (200 l) of water. Piranhas are attracted to blood because they prefer to prey on sick or injured animals.

TERRIBLE TEETH

In this close-up of a red-bellied piranha's mouth, you can see its sharp, triangular teeth.

Piranhas have strong jaws lined with razor-sharp teeth. The teeth are triangular and only about the size of a pencil eraser. Even though they are small, a piranha's teeth are sharp enough to cut through bone! When a piranha's mouth is closed, the teeth on the top and bottom jaws fit together perfectly. If a piranha loses a tooth, a new one will grow in its place.

Piranhas attack by taking grape-sized bites out of their prey. They swallow each bite whole without chewing. Piranhas will continue quickly biting and swallowing until there is nothing left to eat.

SCARY FACTS

1 Native people in South America have used piranha teeth as tools and weapons for thousands of years.

2 Piranhas do an important job as **scavengers** by eating dead animals that have drowned during the yearly floods.

3 Piranhas have been caught in Texas as well as other states. People who keep piranhas as pets sometimes **illegally** release them into streams or lakes in the United States.

4 Red piranhas can **communicate** with sounds, including low grunts and teeth snapping. These sounds are usually used to warn other piranhas to stay away.

5 Piranhas often **ambush** their prey by hiding or staying still until a smaller fish comes close and then attacking suddenly.

6 Piranhas are more dangerous out of the water than in it. People who catch piranhas while fishing are sometimes bitten by them.

7 *Banjo Piranha* is a video game in which the player controls a friendly piranha and tries to collect as many banjos as he or she can.

8 In the 2010 3-D horror movie, *Piranha*, giant, man-eating piranhas attack tourists at a resort.

HUNTING TOGETHER

There are some species of piranhas that swim alone, but most live in schools, or **shoals**. A shoal of piranhas usually has 20 to 30 fish but may contain as many as 300.

Here is a shoal of piranhas swimming together.

When starving piranhas attack prey as a group, you can see the splashing it causes on the water's surface. This is what people call a feeding frenzy.

Piranhas work together when they hunt. Often one piranha will charge a school of smaller fish. When the fish scatter, the other piranhas in the shoal will chase and eat them.

When piranhas go after larger prey, they all attack the animal at once, taking bite after bite. Piranhas may accidentally bite other piranhas. The quick-moving piranhas make the river look like boiling water.

MORE THAN MEAT

Most piranhas are **carnivores**. They do not often kill and eat large mammals, though. Many piranhas prey on smaller fish. They may also eat frogs, insects, birds, and **rodents**. Some kinds of piranhas take bites from other fish's tails and fins and do not even kill their prey. There are also piranhas that eat animals that are already dead.

Discus fish, like the one shown here, are another carnivorous South American freshwater fish. They eat some of the same foods that piranhas do.

Baby anacondas, like the ones shown here, may become prey for a shoal of piranhas.

Piranhas are not just meat eaters. Some species of piranhas eat plants as well as fruit and seeds that fall into the water. Often baby piranhas begin their lives by eating plants.

PROTECTIVE PARENTS

Piranhas **mate** during the rainy season. The female piranha then lays up to 5,000 eggs in a bowl-shaped nest that she digs in the bottom of a lagoon or in a slow-moving part of the river. The male guards the eggs for the next few days, until they hatch. Sometimes the female helps, too.

Baby piranhas stay in the nest and live off the **yolk sacs** from their eggs for about a week. When they leave the nest, they hide among the weeds and eat plants and insects. It takes about a year for a piranha to reach its adult size.

As the young piranhas grow, they go from eating plants and insects to eating larger prey.

PREDATOR AND PREY

Piranhas have many **predators**, especially when they are young. Birds, fish, dolphins, turtles, and otters all eat piranhas. Piranhas may also prey on each other, especially when other food is scarce. People in South America also eat piranhas. Most predators attack from behind to avoid the piranha's sharp teeth.

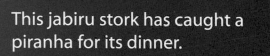

This jabiru stork has caught a piranha for its dinner.

Top: Caimans are relatives of alligators and crocodiles. They are another piranha predator. *Bottom*: The giant otter is a river otter that lives in South America and feeds mostly on fish. This one has just caught a piranha.

Piranhas are most likely to get eaten toward the end of the dry season. Ponds and lagoons may be very small by this time. The piranhas that are trapped in these ponds are weak from hunger and lack of **oxygen**. This makes them easy prey for large birds and mammals.

PIRANHAS AND PEOPLE

While piranhas have bitten people and some people have even lost fingers and toes, no one has ever been attacked by a group of them. People in South America frequently wade and swim in rivers where piranhas live. They know that piranhas will attack people only if they are starving or if they smell blood.

People outside of South America enjoy seeing piranhas at public aquariums. Some people even keep piranhas as pets!

Piranhas are popular attractions at aquariums around the world.

GLOSSARY

ambush (AM-bush) To attack by surprise from a hiding place.

carnivores (KAHR-neh-vorz) Animals that eat only other animals.

communicate (kuh-MYOO-nih-kayt) To share facts or feelings.

illegally (ih-LEE-gul-ee) Unlawfully.

mate (MAYT) To come together to make babies.

oxygen (OK-sih-jen) A gas that has no color or taste and is necessary for people and animals to breathe.

predators (PREH-duh-terz) Animals that kill other animals for food.

prey (PRAY) An animal that is hunted by another animal for food.

rodents (ROH-dents) Animals with gnawing teeth, such as mice.

scavengers (SKA-ven-jurz) Animals that eat dead things.

shoals (SHOHLZ) Large groups of fish, like piranhas.

species (SPEE-sheez) One kind of living thing. All people are one species.

yolk sacs (YOHK SAKS) Bag-like parts inside eggs that hold the yolk, the liquid that feeds the growing baby animal.

INDEX

WEBSITES

Due to the changing nature of Internet links, PowerKids Press has developed an online list of websites related to the subject of this book. This site is updated regularly. Please use this link to access the list:
www.powerkidslinks.com/mak/piran/